ADVANCE PRAISE

I0459287

"Poetry has the power to save the world, and as we witness the unraveling of our present, Rocio offers deep insight into both the personal and the political. These poems speak to the human condition, our faith, and the possibility of finding God within ourselves. As you move through the collection, you are invited to reflect on your own challenges and, in doing so, discover what it truly means to live a purposeful life."

Yosimar Reyes, Author & Performer; 2024 Santa Clara County Poet Laureate; 2024 San José Creative Ambassador

---

"Untying You From Me is a powerful collection of poems that unearth the beauty and the bruises of faith, and belonging. The author transforms lived experience into art that stings, heals, and refuses to be silenced. This is poetry for anyone who has ever carried the weight of otherness and dared to break free."

Gerardo Ivan Morales, Co-Author of Detained *(Simon & Schuster, 2025)*

"This gave me chills. Wow! This was a really powerful piece. I can see how you were taught by fear, not by comfort and love....as someone who struggled with obsessive thoughts before finding peace through faith, this really resonated with me. It captures that inner dissonance in a way that's raw but clear, and I think it will speak to many others who've lived through something similar.... Painful and raw. Very well written....Every one of your poems carries a powerful message—rich with vulnerability yet unafraid in its boldness."

Chester Bolton, Author and Beta Reader

"Survivors of religious trauma, this book is for you. With Untying You From Me, Rocio Flores hasn't just written a poetry anthology—she's created a roadmap from brokenness to healing and empowerment. Capturing raw stories from her own life, through lyrical verses and vivid imagery, Rocio's words will leave you feeling seen. More than that, you will walk away encouraged by the knowledge that healing is attainable and possible. That you can breathe freely and learn to trust yourself fully. If you've ever felt like questioning harmful things is wrong or that your trauma doesn't matter, Rocio's words will remind you: your experiences are real and your healing matters."

Shari A Smith, writer at Running on Faith and Coffee *& co-host of* Survivors Discuss Podcast

---

"A fantastic book....I like the recurring theme of "being." It's linear in the way that we can see emotions evolving in real-time, and I adore that....the majority of readers will absolutely relate to the feelings described. Flores does a great job of letting us see and feel the darkness they do, but also bringing us back up to the light again, so it doesn't feel hopeless."

Kristen Jewel, Author of More Than Half-Drowning *and Beta Reader*

"A powerful and resonating poetic path from silence to empowerment... A striking blend of poetic vulnerability and strength, this book will stay with you long after the final page."

Vanessa Dreme, Editor of Inside My Brain & Wildflower *and Beta Reader*

"A beautiful but heartbreaking collection of poems. Rocio really captures how insidious trauma can be and how resilient we are as human beings."

Natalie Roberts, Author of Write Through Depression, *number 1 Bestseller in Mental Health on Amazon*

"Freedom is possible, even after silence and pain. Untying You From Me unravels generational trauma and systemic injustice with honesty and faith, revealing a path toward love, resilience, and healing. A collection for every soul longing to be unbound and fully seen."

Anne Kinsey, author of Mosaic Hearts: Poems on Being a Queer and Interracial Family in the South

---

"The journey of self-exploration doesn't have to lead to destruction. As these poems show, it can be a path to freedom. Las palabras de Untying You From Me son poemas de libertad."

Rebecca Wilson, Author of Unraveling: Coming Out and Back Together

---

"This book took me through a deeply personal journey of healing. It reminded me that pain and growth often walk hand in hand. If you are moving through hard times, feeling like no one could possibly understand, read this. You'll find pieces of yourself in its words and the quiet comfort of knowing you are not alone."

Velu Ochoa, Musician and Founder, Owner, and Executive Producer of Latinas Be Like Us

---

"This collection is a vulnerable, honest depiction of pain alchemized into healing. Anyone who is navigating mental health struggles, trauma healing, or exploring their faith will find something to connect to in these pages".

Aubree Henderson, Self-Love Coach and Co-Author of Breaking Up With People-Pleasing: Is That Okay?

"A moving and deeply personal journey into loving oneself. Rocio weaves healing and accepting the parts that helped us survive with releasing relationships that no longer contribute to our story in an impressive debut collection."

Dr. Raja Gopal Bhattar, Author of Queering Constellations

"When I read your poems, I don't just see lines. I see wounds. I see moments I've lived through too.... it's not just about relating. It's about feeling less alone in the kind of silence that doesn't have words. Thanks for not pretending. You reminded me that I don't have to either."

Elizabeth Savannah Shelton, Writer and Beta Reader

"The collection is of a woman detailing important events from her past and her journey towards healing. It shows her journey of developing a new mindset and breaking out of old habits. It shows her working through toxic religious views and teachings to develop a relationship with God. It also shows a mother trying to give her son a strong foundation."

Destiny Joy Wells, Beta Reader

Untying You From Me

A Poetry Collection On Being Set Free to Be

Rocio B. Flores

Copyright © 2025

All rights reserved.

No part of this book may be reproduced in any form or by any electronic or
mechanical means, including information storage and retrieval systems, without
written permission from the author, except for the use of brief quotations in a book
review.

Tehom Center Publishing is a 501(c)3 nonprofit publishing feminist and queer
authors, with a commitment to elevate BIPOC writers. Its face and voice is Rev. Dr.
Angela Yarber.

Paperback ISBN: 978-1-966655-50-3

Ebook ISBN: 978-1-966655-51-0

To my son:

Privilege is a tool that can be used to help liberate those without power and empower them to liberate themselves and onward.

You are the fruit of a very long-suffering but enduring tree. You get to break free from the main trunk and sprout a life of your own. You are FREE. I am so excited for you and all the possibilities you get to have in your life. I can't wait to see who you choose to become. I want, so badly, to give you a life free from the pain and hurt that I, and many of our ancestors, have experienced and I also hope and wish that you want to live a life that helps others find that same freedom.

While I would very much like to hide the uglier parts of my life story from you, I'd rather you become a person who is aware of the realities of life and who has a clear connection to someone with these lived experiences so that you can learn to listen to the many others who will one day share their stories with you. I hope you feel my same passion for making sure those stories are told. I wish for you to have a life that allows for this freedom.

I love you so much more than I ever thought was possible.

CONTENT WARNING:

This collection contains themes that may be distressing to some readers, including:

- Emotional, physical, and generational abuse including sexual assault.
- Poverty and systemic inequality.
- Mental health struggles, including references to suicidal ideation.
- Anger, trauma, and societal critique.
- Exploration of faith and spirituality.

These themes are presented with honesty and care, not to sensationalize, but to honor the lived experience of healing. Readers are encouraged to approach the collection with mindfulness and prioritize their emotional well-being.

CONTENTS

LOOSED

FOREWORD

JOSHUA SEEMATTER

I met Rocio when she was a senior in high school. She signed up for Competitive Speech, which was the course from which the Speech and Debate team was formed. Initially, I was not sure that she would make it through the year because she was fairly reserved and soft-spoken; however, there was a fierceness in her eyes. She indicated early in the semester that she was interested in performing poetry, and from that point onward, Rocio and poetry have been synonymous in my mind. The two would not ever be *untied*. During some of her earliest performances, Rocio's diminutive posture and presence were radically juxtaposed with the power of her voice and the words she was saying. Something came alive or came back to life that year. For so long, the ideas and perspectives inside of her did not have a way to get out and be heard; performing poetry became an avenue for her. Poetry was inside of her; it just needed a way to get out. Rocio was very successful in performing that year. What is even more impressive is that she used her passion for the event to become one of the strongest supporters and recruiters for the team. She wanted everyone she knew to have the opportunity she did. Her collection of poetry does something similar in that it puts on display her journey of healing to help others to begin their own. She writes about her lived experience to help others. She fearlessly puts her work into the world, so her son may one day be stronger and more courageous than she can imagine.

After leaving high school, Rocio followed politics and global affairs more closely, and during the COVID-19 Pandemic and subsequent lockdown, she started writing poetry again. As she will tell anyone, it took her a long time to be comfortable with the idea that other people might read her poetry. She had long been a very strong writer as she went through high school and college, but those were merely academic writings - her poetry was a glimpse at her past, mind, journey, and heart. She spent so long and so much time working on becoming a stronger person that to be vulnerable felt wrong; however, as she's coming to terms with the fact that these poems are going to be read by the world, she is confronting her fears. There is strength and courage in her vulnerability.

I wish each of you had the opportunity to meet Rocio one day. To have a conversation with her about what is going on during that particular time of year. You would quickly realize that her mind never stops. She cares so much about what goes on in the world around her, and the compassion she has for others is unbelievable. From education to politics to humanitarian issues, Rocio pays attention, and she does not tout her own beliefs on any particular subject; she asks questions of others. Her knowledge and perspective are not only formed from her own lived experience; rather, she develops a comprehensive view of what is happening and makes connections between things that seemed disparate while discussing with friends, family, loved ones, and sometimes, even strangers. The vantage points Rocio sees in these conversations enable her to have a robust outlook, and when needed, she will selflessly carry the burdens of others.

Her words will simultaneously challenge and support you. They are raw and poignant. They will make you feel uncomfortable and draw you in. You will reflect and feel and think. This collection will take you on a journey that will not end when you have reached the final page because the lasting impact will change the way you reckon with the world and the people you encounter.

Acknowledgments

In fourth grade, I was given a paper certificate saying that I would be a future poet. Let me be clear: I understood that this was just an assignment, and that everyone in class got a decorated paper telling them that they were good at something. I'm part of the participation trophy generation, after all, but that encouragement mattered. I can't say I remember that teacher's name, but I remember how seen I felt. I'm grateful for that teacher, and the many more teachers, therapists, and mentors who have taken the extra step to really see me. Thank you.

I can't say I genuinely believed I would ever become a real poet. So much of my writing has happened late at night, scribbled on hidden pages of notebooks, in fear that anyone might ever see my words. The fact that I even get to share this book means so much to me. I'm incredibly grateful for everyone who has been a part of my journey, not just in writing this book, but in helping me become the kind of person who would even attempt to do it.

First and foremost: thank you, Tony. I love you. We've talked a lot about how our lives could have been so different if we hadn't gotten married so young. We have helped each other stay on a path different from the generations before us. You have been my main supporter, my best friend, and my foundation. I feel so incredibly blessed to have a man like you in my life. Thank you, baby.

To my church family: I fear that if I hadn't agreed to go to church with my mother-in-law that first time I walked into Waypoints, I may have never truly found Jesus. Walking into a room full of people, interacting with, eating with, and loving every kind of person there — the unhoused, the mothers, the children, and those definitely not dressed in "church attire" like me — helped me decide to keep learning and searching. I feel that without this community, I would have fallen away from seeking God, or worse, fallen into a religious prison unaligned with Christ's vision for the Kingdom. Every Friday night meal keeps me sane and alive.

The first few months after having my child were really difficult, and I want to thank the people who helped me. Some of you came to my house, or let me be in yours, and just sat with me, fed me, talked to me, and some of you even sat with my baby in hospital waiting rooms. My mom literally stayed on video call with me all day, every day, so I would never be alone. Without you, I don't think I would be here today.

Gracias a mis padres. Our lives have been very hard. I know the legacy we carry, and I understand how parents have to make difficult decisions based solely on the information and resources they have at the moment. I know you loved us, and you both dealt with life as best as you could while carrying so much of your own trauma, pain, and harm. Because of your bravery and the generational knots you broke loose, I have been able to raise my child, unchained. I love you both so much, and I am grateful for the relationship we've been able to build today and for the loving grandparents that you are.

I want to thank every individual who took time out of their busy schedules to read this book and endorse it, including all of the wonderful writers at Tehom Center Publishing. I want to thank everyone at TCP for believing in this book and in me, for encouraging and pushing me, and for all of the hard work you do to make sure that every kind of voice has a chance to be heard.

And last but not least, my little baby boy (sorry, BIG BOY). I want so much for you, and I want you to see me be as much as I can be for you. I want my faith to influence yours. I want my work to encourage yours. I want my love to increase yours. You are my lifeline. God's biggest gift.

Thank you, Lord, for this blessing.

THREADLESS

"For the wages of sin is death"

— ROMANS 6:23

"In the spaces between nothing, there is everything."

— UNKNOWN

"Surely I spoke about things I did not understand,
  things too wonderful for me to know."

— JOB 42:3

Poem 1: A thread unraveled...

My mom used the Devil
to teach me my lessons.
Don't touch kitchen knives!
—what if—he MAKES you...

...cut into yourself. —what if—
Don't get too close to the sidewalk!
...walk into traffic! —what if—
You could...you *Could*...

She told me a tale,
of God and the Devil,
knitting a sweater;
a child's parable.

God grabbed his yarn,
just enough as he needed,
patiently building,
minute by minute.

The devil pulled and pulled
and pulled. —Greedy.
Until there he sat in a mess;
knots, ties. Useless threads.

Don't be like him,
she warned.
Learn your lesson.
Never test him!

She taught me about God,
about Jesus, Grace and Sin;
but Satan stayed with me.
The threads had unfurled within.

Don't test him;
by trusting yourself.
It was too late.
I let him in.

What if—what if
What if
What.
If.

Poem 2: Be Seen Not Heard

I was taught;
Be Seen and Not Heard.
For to speak is to
choose. —violence.

For trying, I learned;
that using my voice
means taking a risk.
slapped, kicked. —broken.

I've been insulted. —silenced.
I learned to be careful when
speaking. Heed to authority!
To people's emotional reactivity…

I learned to use my voice
to stay safe. —manipulate.
To put my discomfort at the helm
of other people's will. —violence.

Destroy any sense of self identity
for the sake of false security.
I dare not intimidate, because
I know what real intimidation is.

I've learned now,
it was NOT my voice;
it was NOT my choice.
THEIR fear was the reason.

Emotions were triggered.
Their discomfort. —pain.
Their cowardice. —fear.
Their lack of power, —over me.

I will use my voice now;
regardless, heedless. —seen.
I will use it and I will teach them
to deal with their own hiding.

Poem 3: OCD

If all that's wrong with me
is thoughts,
then I just want it fixed.
I don't need to think.

My fear is there is nothing wrong
and I'll always have to be like this.
I'd much rather be a careless person
than an anxious one...

but the thoughts
don't
LET
me.

Thinking nothing at all
sounds so nice.
A pretty little fool?
Joyful Cluelessness...

just a fool, instead.
Overcrowded musings.
Lackadaisical intrusions,
weighing down my heart...

——

I feel like everything I know is wrong.
I live in constant dissonance. —Hevel
I've been in a game since I left home
and I can't figure out how to finish it.

I
should
Finish
it...

Poem 4: I wish I had scowled

I wish most of all
that I wasn't smiling in pictures
where I didn't feel like it.

I was more concerned with
what thoughts my frown might
conjure in –them,

than with honoring
the thoughts that were
eating away at –me,

behind
the
lens,

behind the veneer
of my hidden
shame. —Unseen.

Poem 5: My Misgivings

Reaching my arms to his neck,
seeking to still the feelings of fear
of too young a little girl,
making decisions unhealed.

He grabbed my arms —gently,
set them to the side, out of his way.
A breathless "I love you"
I wheezed out, unmeant

...to make special
a moment that hurt me,
even more than the next;
when I said NO
and he didn't care...

when, I wasn't mentally there,
and I could soothe myself quietly,
pretend to be well and good:
coy, and couth. —Willing.

With hands to my side
—knowing my place.
Touching his neck
was my mistake.

Poem 6: My House Will Be

My house was pain,
fear reigned.

A lack of freedom
—persisted.
A grasp for air
—resisted.

I was tired.
12 and done with life.
I was angry.
15 and ready to end it.

I was quiet.
17 and done thinking.
I was sad.
18 and done hoping.

I was then
22 and still crying…
25 and still seeking…
28 but still trying…

—

I am 32 now—
sleeping, resting,
talking, building,
—reaping.

My house is joy,
speaking —encouraged.
Hatred —thwarted.
Freedom —chosen.

—living.

Poem 7: No One Is Listening

I want to talk. To share,
all the random thoughts
my brain makes me
listen to.

I want to share my theories.
I want to find people who agree,
that we can change the world,
that I can make myself free.

If I can share my ideas
on how to do it,
what's stopping me?
Who can judge me?

I can talk:
–forget the pain
–forget the hurt
no one is stopping me…

I am talking!
I have been.
Why can't they
hear me…?

–Forget the lies.
–Forget the faking.
–Forget the mediocrity.
Show the world!

Just say IT!
Make them LOOK!
But don't, STOP!
Don't do it...

Stop yourself.
Be realistic.
Who are you kidding?
No one is listening.

Poem 8: Please Listen

Listen
and pay attention
because
i'm not saying what
I want to say.

There's a coded message
in my eyes and
my fingertips.

Notice my foot shaking
and the slight tremors.
Notice my gaze
and half smile,
—my polite gestures.

I'm telling you
I need help.
Please listen.

I don't want to keep
hiding …see me.
Seek and feel
what I am living.
Apply your heart.
Tune your ear.

Please Listen—
Hear what you
can't hear—

UNRAVELING

"You reveal the path of life to me."

— *PSALM 16:11*

"We are not meant to be fixed; we are meant to be lost and found."

— *UNKNOWN*

"A time to tear and a time to mend, a time to be silent and a time to speak."

— *ECCLESIASTES 3:7*

Poem 9: The Angels

I was like the angels I drew as a kid,
perfect and clean and One with You.
But I let the darkness in. . .

clouding
my
innocence.

The thoughts came in…
and made me see myself
—undeserving.

God, how do I know
if these years were just a trial?
Maybe this is the path to You?

There were a lot of obstacles.
I went through —evil —hell —fear.
Each one because I care

so much to see, You.
Born of You —redeemed.
One with You —whole.

—

I once feared for my life,
then I feared living, then
I didn't fear death, enough.

Now I fear the future.
I fear remembering.
I fear

       not
                  finding

         You.

I fear finding myself.

Poem 10: I want to be

I stopped reading
when I realized each letter
brought me closer

to the end
of one world
and back to m

i
n
e.

I started writing because
I could just put
—anonymous—

at the end of my
confessions and
no one could

know
my
selfishness.

I want to complain
to the world,
I want to

tell them that
I want it to stop.
I want it ALL to stop.

I just want to feel normal.
I want to read again.
I want to be—

but how?
Fruitless
end of story.

Fruitless
end of
me.

Poem 11: Just Be Happy

I should "just be happy"
:motto of my life,
unfortunately fortunate,
how dare I cry?

Weeping for a self;
how selfish is that?
People are dying:
hungry, nameless.

I was fed. I was loved,
mostly.
Controlled and protected?
I was told, —blessed.

The journey to selfhood,
a first-world conquest...
Is it? A colonized mindset
sounds more like it.

"They didn't know better"...
I believe that.
It's been my job to teach them.
A journey in itself.

Thankless work;
but worthy.
My worth,
self —Less.

Poem 12: Mediocrity

Oh, mediocrity...
what I could have
been
but was
not.

The accolades of youth,
a construction paper certificate
printed with good meaning;
saying go for it,
You Can Do It!

You and 34 other students...
A future Poet,
an Astronaut,
a President,
a well adjusted human?

Best to focus on customer service,
and throw in some sales.
A call center will take bilinguals!
A real estate agent, perhaps?
The Avon lady, if you're into that...

A warehouse distribution manager
pays well enough;
just don't end up in jail,
or do drugs...
make a few bucks!

Pay all of your bills.
Stay sober!
That's way more than
was expected–
from the kid who thought they'd

 become a poet
 after writing a miscount'd
 haiku in fourth grade.

Poem 13: Please Save Me

back in queue,
back in anger;
annoyed at the world—
addicted to its favors.

searching for god,
hoping for magic;
take away the demands—
God, please help me.

afraid of consequences,
beliefs too powerful;
unable to change me—
not trying hard enough.

angry at myself,
for reasons in my heart;
unwilling to try—
the changes seem so hard.

upset about the world,
don't know how to escape;
help me leave here—
help me renounce it.

lead me on the right path,
lead me not astray;
rebuke the horror—
rebuke the pain.

help me.
i'm afraid.
rebuke the power.
please God, save me.

Poem 14: A Mule

My dad used to call me
a mule.
It meant to mean I was
stubborn
—like my mother.

The mother who fought
to survive for ten years
—and finally left him.

I was okay with being
THAT kind of stubborn.
Unfortunately
my stubbornness grew
in a different direction.

      I was so scared of being like them.

I didn't want to be
like my father,
—abusive.

I didn't want to yell,
or be mean,
or cause fear.
I didn't want ANY
power.

      So I did the opposite!

I stayed silent.
I cowered.
I let people use words I didn't like;

words that shouldn't have been mine.
Made myself to be small
—to survive.
Resolved to stay in my place,
unmovable;

for FAR too long...

Year after year,
through hard lessons I learned,
that being small
wouldn't make people
—love me;

but this lesson,
i kept on repeating
...like a mule.

Until the day I gave up
the expectation that somehow
making myself small
could reconcile my
—intention;

that holding firm
in my smallness
was virtuous…

instantly, I got the answer I needed.

Painful validation but
validation indeed. I was rewarded
for being willing to let go
of my fear of being mean.
No longer being stubborn —discerning.

I read up on mule caretaking…
when they're well led
and taken care of,
      they're not stubborn…
            they're Strong.

Never again will it take years.
I can be stubborn IN THIS.
Tomorrow I'll break these chains...
for now, I'm unwilling to be
whipped during the wait.

Poem 15: A Thing

I've always carried a story in my mind,
a narrative of my experience...
my way of processing
—the chaos.

I've had a lot of experiences.
I felt, and physically was,
disconnected from
—my body.

I used to feel stuck,
incapable of escaping,
decisions made
—by others.

I was unable to push
past my own fears,
and often... without
—a choice;

or even
awareness
it was possible;
—my choice.

I made myself a Thing.
A thing to be dictated to.
A thing to be molded.
An object to vilify and bully.

I, myself, shared in
my own dehumanization.
I may have not started it but
I made certain I'd be the main actor;

a very
powerful
coping
mechanism.

It brought me out
from under,
someone else's rule; into
—my own.

I made myself a thing
that I would not let
anyone else use except
—for myself.

Today, I am a Person.
A human being.
A Child of God.
I am not a thing.

I notice in me
the pull of force,
when I am not
—being me;

the discomfort
of dismissal,
the ease of
conformity.

When I step outside
of my body,
the bubbling tears;
—of courage.

I remember then,
that God catches
each droplet.
I will cry.

I will no longer
not BE.
I will speak.
I will scream.

Because I AM no longer a thing.

Poem 16: My Weakness

My whole life
I've had to be strong.
Strong enough to withstand
Violence:

physical,
emotional,
and mental
Violence.

So a wall of protection I built
around my heart, my mind,
and my hope. I survived,
but never thrived...

Fearfully, I took steps,
one at a time, carefully
and with an eye looking
over my shoulder,

towards the promises
of safety
and comfort.
Promises of Being–

Today, I see hope.
I see growth.
I see change.
I see me–

in a vision of a life
I never thought
I could or
would ever live.

I can BE,
and today
I Choose
to Be;

to let my guard down,
because I believe
HIS power is made
perfect in my weakness.

I choose to be
vulnerable,
—free from defense.
Allowing God

to pick up the sword.
Allowing for my heart
to be carried, held
—enjoyed.

Today, I am weak…
because weakness
begets strength;
strength I'll need from now on.

Poem 17: Kintsugi

I still break everyday,
some cracks are big,
some are small.

They hurt.
…but God fills them with gold,
and they mean something.

I mean something.

I never stay broken.
I was born whole,
from dust to Gold.

Imago Dei.
A Refined Talent.
Worthy Resolve.

Poem 18: No Flowers

We didn't have flowers growing up.
No picture frames on the wall.
Living in unfinished basements,
we used buckets as toilet bowls.

In that one cellar we stayed in,
we didn't even have buckets.

These aren't things people care
to share about their lives.
How embarrassing to say that
we had roaches and bed bugs.

I sharpied my legs black
to cover holes in my pants.
When you run out of TP,
free newspapers work just fine…

I have a lot of these stories.
I have others as well;

How I made paper costumes
for Halloween and for Christmas.
I would draw snowflakes and our tree.
Mami used floss to sew doll clothes—free.

I learned to collect precious things
and to give value to pure imagination.

I didn't feel poor.
I didn't think about having more.
I thought about being free
and wanting just to breathe.

Today, I mentioned to my mom
how it wouldn't have mattered
if we had had a big house,
decorations, or "success markers."

We didn't have air. A fake stuffed image.
I have air now, God breathes through me.

I go to the store for .99¢ plants to revive...
decorate —innovate— Dollar Tree "junk."
I make intricate paper snowflakes designs.
My walls are filled —pictures —drawings.

I sit by my window during sunshine hour,
no need to fake a happy home...
I have the freedom to choose how I live.
I've made my home my own.

I don't drive a Tesla.
I won't buy an iPhone.
I shop deals and
I live for the thrift store.

No name brands,
and no fear.

I've made my days —my freedom.
I've made my love —my air.
I'm not ashamed of my past lack.
We fix our gaze on the unseen...

I thank God for every glint
of sunlight on my plants —on me.

To those wanting to see
ONLY the world,
my world doesn't seem like much;
maybe we should want "more"...

but I feel abundant in hope,
in safety, —inspired
in gratitude, —seen
everlasting joy. Rich indeed.

Tangled

"You yourselves do not enter, nor will you let those enter who are trying to."

— Matthew 23:13

"La rabia es el amor que no ha sido escuchado."

— Unknown

"Hatred stirs up strife, but love covers all sins."

— Proverbs 10:12

Poem 19: These Messages

We receive messages in our life
that shape us,
some from those that raised us,
some from those raised along us.

Some come with
a promise of help,
to leave our upbringing;
unindentured support...

Sometimes we don't realize that,
in our quest to reject what is wrong,
we allow what seems innocent
...to take over.

Hurt
is easy to see.
Harm
is hard to notice.

I was taught violence,
impulse, and fear.
Those ideas are hard to change
but easy to perceive.

...but the messages
I ran to
haven't always been
easy to shed.

My worth and WHO
gets to determine it...
who gets to choose
what is right and what isn't?

Who gets to tell me
HOW to live?
Who gets to shape
MY experiences?

Who
gets to
LIKE
me?...

It's easy to KNOW
that a person who
physically harms you,
isn't showing you LOVE;

it's not as easy to recognize
that a person who demands
that you submit to their will,
for you to get their love, is ALSO

not
showing
you
love.

New types of fears,
these messages taught me:
of losing relationships,
retaliation,

of not being loved, being Me.

Shaking, trembling,
and sweating,
overt fear;
is easy to see.

Avoidance, discomfort,
and pain,
unseen but felt;
when someone is

using their love
as a weapon
against
me.

These messages try to teach
that only overt fear is real.
Unless someone is hitting you,
you don't have a right to feel...

You have to take
whatever comes at you,
to KEEP their love.
It's not about us. Me, or You.

These messages are worse.
It's violence wrapped
in a bow that chokes you
and leaves you

surrounded by people
that don't like you,
and when you leave,
won't even miss YOU.

Poem 20: These Times

Am I crazy? Am I free?
Marginalized, weak? Unseen.
Awake and mad, or

alone and falling...
        deeper and deeper
               and further into *silence.*

The silence of "the times"
the times to come,
the times I see and understand,

the times I already know
I can't affect, and
probably won't withstand.

Suppressed. Unfree.
These times, you say,
are "just in my head"...

I won't privy you to
the visions that are
actually there,

                    you don't care.

"They won't do that!"
They might,
they do.

"It can't happen here!"
It has, it does,
it's true!

Thousands frozen
on snowy streets;
empty building in the scene.

Babies crying,
their mother's defeat.
It wasn't their choice, you see.

Laws, they say,
laws for who?
Laws for me, not you.

Paid-for lockups.
Paid-for immunity.
Paid-for ignorance.

My people's fear,
your people's "security"...
Silence! Sleep!

I won't lose sleep
but I might take a nap.
I can't keep going...

but I also can't stop.
I can't do this alone.
I don't have the "right" voice.

I am crazy and paranoid,
asleep and forlorn;
not quite gone,

but not quite not.
I guess I'll keep going.
At least I can say that I fought.

Poem 21: Revival

Why is it always us that are wrong?
Why are we always the ones
that have to question *our* hearts?

Why do we have to
be nice,
to be safe?

Why do we have to be silent,
to be listened to?
Why must we change *our* language,

but you won't assess yours?
Why are we angry,
but you are "righteous"?

Why must we repress and submit,
while you suppress and deny?
Why are we always **tired** while you are

—revived

Poem 22: Herejes

No entienden,
o nos ven como marcianos,
o morenos assimilados.
Gringos a SU estilo

—nunca Mexicanos.

Criminales o
acceptables,
nunca
humanos.

Borren sus memoria,
levanten la bandera
correcta!
O assimilense…

al sonido del miedo,
al callar,
al nunca llamarle a Dios,
en nuestro idioma.

Somos herejes
si le lloramos a nuestro Padre,
en nuestra tierra.
Herejes, por implorarle

sobre este
cielo compartido.
Pecadores,
por buscar asilo.

Pecadores por querer derechos,
justicia,
perdon,
—vecinos.

Diosito, dales ojos que busquen
vernos, reales,
humanos, vivos,
—hermanos en tu destino.

Poem 23: Yet

You are not
    better than
        "that person"...

The one who did *that*
horrible thing you think
you would NEVER do.

Especially not when, statistically
you are the prime demographic
of people that choose to

do the evil things you swear
people are going to Hell for.
—Judgement.

You are not more human,
or more inherently worthy
of considering your life choices.

Nor are you more intelligent,
or clever, or have better
willpower.

You just haven't done
the thing they have done,
—yet.

You haven't been forced,
or coerced,
or manipulated,

or found yourself stuck, at a loss,
without the ability to see
beyond your current choices.

You
are not
different.

You
are
lucky.

Extend your luck to them,
step on the line
to actually make a difference,

or
        look

             down.

Look at your feet,
walk in the shame,
you throw at others.

You're not doing
what you think you are…
That shame of yours;

it can't make their decisions easier,
it can't give them more options,
it can't make them do what

you haven't
HAD to choose
to do. —yet.

You walk in your sin.
They haven't chosen your sin, and
you just haven't chosen theirs —yet.

Feel the luck
that has kept you
from that choice.

Rejoice in the Grace
that's been *gifted,*
to you **both**.

Poem 24: Me Too

I don't want to fit into
"categories."
I don't want to be
"unafraid."

I want to not have
had to
be afraid
in the first place—

Why should I choke it down,
pretend to be strong,
and then have to fight,
for it to be gone?

It wasn't my fault.
Why aren't
you
doing "the work?"

Why is it always
"me too?"
When this was all
just because of you.

Poem 25: Walk Away

I get this buzzing feeling
throughout my body;
pressure in my stomach,
nausea and a burn.

My head pounds;
my chest feels heavy.
Everything is loud and
lights everywhere, too many.

Too many colors, too many thoughts...
I feel afraid... I feel like running,
but where is it safe?
I don't know because...

—*it's not clear...*

The lack of clarity,
unwillingness to be direct,
the subtle and veiled insults,
calls to unity; calls to submit.

The calls for peace,
those are scariest...
they send chills down my spine.
Where do they stand?

and would they stand for me?

If I was running for my life
would I be told;
I just need to
breathe?

When they take mild stances;
they are only
protecting
themselves.

People can't be called out
when using "nice" words...
you'll be the jerk if you
dare ask them to be firm.

"angry"...
"fearful"...
"offended"...
..."faithless"

You'll be typecast
and they'll get praise.
Who doesn't praise
the appearance of peace?

Find safe places.
Places you can cry
without the fear of offending;
that's what I've learned so far...

Take care of your body:
breathe, move, drink water,
pray,
and lament;

because there's lamenting to do...
"Who's going to speak up?"
"What are we going to do?"
–Judges 19:30

Call on God, but also,
walk away,
from places that aren't meant
for you, places that refuse

to
become
for
you.

Poem 26: My Best

I can only do MY best.
I can't do my husband's or my son's,
my mother/father/brother/sister's
best. I am not them.

I can advocate for others.
I can motivate others.
I can influence others.
I can demand of others.

But I am not, OTHERS.
I am me.
I do what I am able to do each
week, day, and moment.

I respond.
I listen.
I decide.
I concede.

I take responsibility for ME.
But that's all
that's IN me.
I won't apologize for it.

Others can apologize
for their own shortcomings...
Others can rise up and
fulfill their own promises...

No longer will I take on
the personhood of
anyone,
that isn't me.

Others could support me too,
but that's not what's
expected of them;
they are not me…

Poem 27: My Needs

I'm using all
of my coping skills
today, because today,
I have needs.

I have a need:
to feel safe,
to feel loved,
to feel wanted,

to feel cared for,
to feel appreciated,
to feel—
free.

Today, I feel the need to
shout from a mountaintop,
that it's not *your* needs
that matter to me;

that I don't need to protect you,
that it's not your vanity,
your image, your facade
—that matters.

It's not your feelings,
your fears,
your life,
that I need to prioritize.

Today, I need a reminder,
to MYSELF:
that I don't need you,
I never did—

I made this life
in spite of you;
I learned all these skills
to protect myself *from* you,

that you didn't care
when I needed you...
Now, I don't have to
choose —YOU.

I will speak
when I need to,
I will share;
MY life, MY story, MY tears,

MY feelings, MY pain,
—your involvement—
regardless of how it makes
YOU feel.

I will be. I will live.
I am my priority.
I won't make you my priority
anymore.

I don't hate you,
but the only love I can give you
today,
is to choose myself,

and disregard your need
for me to be quiet,
chained, and bent
to your will,

because I know that my freedom
can only aid in yours.
That's the only hope I can carry for you.
That's the only need I'll meet for you now.

Today, I won't take your command.
Today, I'm choosing my needs, not yours.
Today, I choose my freedom over yours.
Today, MY need is to NOT need you.

Poem 28: My Needs Pt. 2

I need water
and I need sunshine
and I need music.

I need air
and I need a good book
and I need a good friend.

       I need God.
       I need to pray.
       I need to meditate.

I need to breathe
and I need to write
and I need to paint.

I need to sing
and I need to feel
and I need to cry.

       I need my cat.
       I need my husband.
       I need my child.

I need some good sleep
and some good food
and some Hot Cheetos too.

I need sunshine
and I need full moons
and I need constellations too.

I need silence.
I need noise.
I need to speak.

I need sounds
of love and hope;
of support and joy.

I don't
        need
                you.

LOOSED

"There is no end to the making of many books, and much study wearies the body."

— ECCLESIASTES 12:12

"To grasp the meaning of a self is to let go of the weight that binds it."

— UNKNOWN

"Come to me, all you who are weary and burdened, and I will give you rest."

— MATTHEW 11:28

Poem 29: A Beautiful Life

Fear set in at age 3.
Sleepless nights at 5.
Silence at 7.
Soon came the Thoughts.

Shyness set in
during 5th grade.
A Split started
in middle school.

In 7th grade I learned
not to Believe.
The summer before 8th grade
I began harming myself.

Then I really started
to "rebel"
—or so they said.
Boys became a thing,

but Shame hit
the summer before 10th grade,
and that pain grew and grew,
until I graduated.

I had fought back
the first time, at 17,
but I didn't leave
for good 'till 19.

I sought help at 20, scaredly.
Diagnosed at 22:
a very big list.
I sought God at 25.

Then came doctors
and medications,
books and therapy,
—and Myself…

I lost friends.
I made new ones.
I risked my identity.
I fought like hell.

9 months 'till
some meds kicked in!
3 years 'till
I believed God again..

4 years 'till
I shared my reality.
"Boundaries"
—a book of magic.

I was 28 when
I stood up to my dad,
A pandemic
helped me say many goodbyes;

a lot of people
on that list…
a lot of trusting
to abide by.

My hope was restored at 29;
gave birth
and turned 30.
Now I will go on…

      What a
            Beautiful
                  Life
    …it has been so far.

Poem 30: abNormal

For years my goal in therapy
was to be more *normal.*
Now my goal is
to be more Me.

At first I didn't understand
why I wasn't "like others",
why I always felt
—different.

There is a joke I
wasn't included in.
I wanted more than anything
to just "get it".

        I couldn't.

My goal was to be
as normal as I could.
I wanted to wake up
and FEEL like I was feeling

    What
     Everyone
     Else
    Was.

Wakeup,
live,
"get it",
and Do.

Now I wake up to BE.
I'm not like everyone else.
No one is.
My struggle now is in

BEING

The world tells us
be like others. Fit in.
Strive for what
others strive for…

be **normal.**

BEING ME
requires letting go
of the facade of
—likeability.

I may not be accepted.
and I have to be okay
with that knowing…
I have to be okay

with feeling

wrong

for striving to be

abnormal.

Because striving
to be
normal,
is wrong

for
me
and for
you.

Poem 31: A Guise

I am not a swan.
I am but a duck.
I swim, I fly, and I run…
whatever is needed of me.

I transform to fit their needs…

but I don't really like the water
and I'm afraid of heights. It's cold.
I waddle and quack and waddle
too much—

      Always Too Much…

I'm never what they *want;*
only what they need.
It's never my lake.
The park is too busy.

      I am alone.

Maybe I could be a goose?
Unliked. Unbothered. Hissing.
Maybe I'd get to vamoose.
Maybe they would run from me…

      Just Being Me. Hidden. Free.

I just want to be what I am!
I'm not aiming to be a swan.
The ugly duckling's story sucks!
—to know that you're only loved

      when you fit the mold they want.

Poem 32: The Diary

I was "The Diary;"
the person people came to,
to tell their secrets,
and work out their troubles.

I felt closest to my Dad,
during his midnight rants;
sharing his life with me,
counseling his vulnerabilities.

I was the parent,
the mom of my young friend groups,
the counselor, the advice-giver...
Being needed used to FEEL SO GOOD.

It prompted me
to study psychology.
I noticed patterns
of friendships ending

when I was no longer
the therapist.
No longer the diary,
my pages ended.

There's a difference
between being needed
and being wanted,
liked, enjoyed...

I felt the heaviness of this.
It weighed on me to know,
I couldn't really share myself...
people only cared to share themselves.

Believing that I was
close to people who
did not consider me
close to them, —hurt.

Holding such deep secrets
inside of myself,
unable to share Me,
was killing —myself.

Confirmed fears are scary,
but fear and pain,
are worth learning
how to change patterns.

It IS possible to make friends
that LOVE you;
and show you
you can be

held,
supported,
listened to,
wanted…

ENJOYED.

Poem 33: I Can Do It All

I wasn't taught to rest.
"If you've got time to lean,
you've got time to clean..."
I was taught to work,

      "like you're working for God."

Every step you take should matter.
People are watching.
People will notice.
It is what is "right."

      "Don't let people think badly of you."

Coming into my own life,
I went in with that mentality.
I worked full time,
I went to school.

      "I will be an independent woman!"

Had a side gig.
Did therapy.
Got some dogs.
Became a good wife.

      "I can do it ALL!"

...if I'm having panic attacks every day,
...if I feel like just not living anymore,
...if I hate myself,
...I can do it all...

      "I can't do it at all?"

I couldn't understand how to
DO IT ALL and BE.
How do others do it?
Others can, but only I can't?

"What's wrong with me?"

How do I get clean dishes
AND money
AND be an inspiration
for the whole world?

"I just must be broken."

Made incorrectly.
An image of
laziness;
—mediocrity.

"It will never end."

a new task,
a new project,
a new want,
and a new person to please.

"Stop!"

Take a break.
Step away.
Take a Sabbath.
God gives rest to the weary.

"I am tired."

Learn a lesson from me;
NO ONE DOES IT ALL.
None of us. We weren't meant to,
and the happy few, aren't trying to.

"Sit the fuck down!"

Rest. Sleep.
Society's expectations only serve
to shame us into compliance;
–fruitless servitude…

Poem 34: My Confidence

Yesterday,
in talking about
stepping away from therapy,
I wrote down:

> *"It's hard for me*
> *to feel confident.*
> *That's an area I want*
> *to be better in!"*

I left feeling like I was a bit
TOO confident, arrogant even,
in my stance and belief of how
I WILL hold up from here on.

10 years of therapy…
In the days I started,
confidence was not
ANYWHERE on my radar.

I did NOT like myself.
I did NOT trust myself.
I did NOT believe myself.
I did not WANT to.

I was drifting,
moment to moment,
completely unsure,
un-momentous a future.

So much guilt from the many times
I did not hold myself up.
I genuinely believed deep down
that I was just bad, —evil

hated,
unlovable.
Deserving
of all the hurt...

Now I've done the work,
to prove to myself,
I'm capable of holding
myself up.

I know when
I have an ability,
even better;
I know when I do not.

I know when I am struggling.
I know when I need help.
I know what real support is.
I know when to seek it out.

Getting to this place was not easy,
but it's very much deserved.
It's not arrogant; confident even.
It was worth the work.

Poem 35: The Eye of The Tornado

I've always wanted
either
a completely still
windless day...

or a ravaging tornado
to come through...
and force a calm
devastation to come.

Waiting between
stillness and change,
a windy day is
a reminder of...

the lack of control
I have in this world;
the chaos that I've
always existed in.

But I don't *actually*
want a tornado. . .
I want to sit with
just the wind

and know that with
or without chaos,
all will be okay.
—I will be okay.

It doesn't have to
turn into destruction...
I don't have to
be left with nothing...

I can and will
handle the storms,
and the in-betweens of
—**ME BEING ME.**

Poem 36: Don't Fix Your Face

It used to be hard for me
to share silly faces,
make my own facial expressions
that go beyond smiling stoicism.

i
just
couldn't.
...and I just SWALLOWED that inability.

I grew up in a home where
making the wrong face could
lead to being yelled at
—or worse.

...and it was the person
I felt the least safe with,
that was always the best
at guessing exactly how I felt.

so...I learned to be VERY careful.
It served me well.
It kept me safe.
An honorable skillset, I don't regret.

But I don't want it anymore...
I resigned myself to being
THAT person;
the one who won't

dance in front of others,
or sing, or even
hum or sway...
—or **be**.

I, for a long time, was OKAY
...suppressing…
anything that gave anyone
—power over me...

not even
feeling…
so I wouldn't
SLIP.

I've realized in controlling
how much power another person
could try and wield against me,
I was still being controlled…

I'd been DROWNING
behind a smile
that's only ever kept people
from NOTICING my terror.

… "this is my life"
… "this is what I chose"
… "this is what I have to
—live— with."

—the paralyzing FEAR of what if—
YEARS fighting the ever-present
ugly RISK of dealing with…
unhappy recipients.

It's not really you LIVING
if it's not YOU feeling.
...don't fix your face,
it is not worth

—NOT BEING.

Poem 37: I Grew A Rose

Oh my God,
I grew a ROSE!!!
It's tiny and it didn't
grow from scratch,

but I kept the plant
alive through winter,
watered it with hope,
and a rose finally hatched!

I never thought I'd grow a rose…
I never thought I'd keep one alive.
I thought my home was
where plants came to die.

I thought my heart was concrete,
made to trap all love.
No dreams, no hope, just cracks;
death's destination stop.

I thought I wouldn't live,
no way I could survive.
No way sunshine and water
could penetrate my mind…

but today I'm growing life.
Roots digging deep.
I might actually thrive!
I'm seeing buds bloom,

inside of me
and inside of you.
I finally grew a rose.
…and my cactus is

doing
pretty
good
too...

Poem 38: Let The River Flow

I know who I am, now.
I've questioned myself to determine,
if even the smallest aspects are mine.
What is ME? What isn't?...

I am confident in my knowing
and my unknowing.
I'm committed to still
a whole lifetime of learning.

I know from experience,
that this isn't an easy place to get to.
Many aren't trying; many more
are unaware they can try to..

It's hard to question who you are,
without destroying yourself in the process,
or forcing yourself to be who you are not,
to feel like you've finished faster.

Most people go with the flow, —led
by the current of society, —floating—
becoming whatever is needed of them,
often only recognizing the hate

they've pointed at
themselves,
when turning it towards
others.—

I've memorized this feeling, the way
my bones shake in those moments.
I've worked up the courage to step away,
a great cost of keeping my ground steady.

Many people do the opposite.
They deny. They lie. They avoid it.
They don't swim with the current,
they're dragged…

all hope of autonomy lost.
That feeling...is worse.
It's more forgivable but,
a bigger strain on the soul.

It takes courage to fight the currents;
to ask ourselves where we are going.
To then be willing to part with
anything that needs to GO,

and MORE importantly,
keep a clear conscience;
hold steadfast to the parts of us that
are already there and need protection.

God made ME, with purpose,
and it's been my journey
to LET the person He created, BE.
It's been hard. But worthy.

This journey is NOT easy.
People may JUDGE you —dislike you.
You may be USED as an excuse
for their lack of resolution.

They may see your vulnerability
as a weakness to fix.
They may shame you for being direct
in your own determination, —for being free.

Do it anyway.
BE anyways.
Keep learning.
Keep growing.

The stronger the roots,
the harder to kill.
Extend your flowers to be seen.
Share your fruit.

Let the river flow as it needs to.

YOU just BE you.

Poem 39: Dear Shame and Guilt

Dear Shame and Guilt:
you helped me survive,
and for this,
I am grateful.

You whispered in my ear,
messages aiming
to help me stay safe;
of smallness and deprecation.

You taught me that
I always have a choice
in how to think about the things
happening in front of me —to me.

I could be small and go unnoticed.
I could be quiet and save my face.
I could smile and save others pain.
"Empathy matters more than my vanity."

I didn't need applause or praise.
I could understand others' ways.
You taught me to walk carefully,
tip-toe when on shaky ground.

You helped me to keep from falling.
I now KNOW I can stay safe.
You taught me that I could take control!
I am here, ALIVE, because of it.

You showed me how to strive
for perfection; make no mistakes,
hide the ones I couldn't avoid making.
You did YOUR job! –high stakes.

I thank you so much...*but*
in order for me to KEEP on LIVING,
I think I need you to take a step back...
I need you to STOP.

You'll probably still be
trying to whisper in my ear. . .
I'll probably feel you in my heart.
I don't know how long that will last,

but...today I am ALIVE to KNOW,
that I have enough agency
to take your advice,
or choose a NEW path.

I can choose self-love —compassion.
I can make mistakes —authenticity.
I can choose to acknowledge
my imperfections —humanity.

> Others can
> choose to
> see me
> that way.

I've LEARNED that I am allowed to
make other people uncomfortable,
AND that other people get to deal
with their own discomfort, —or not.

I've DECIDED that I am worthy
of being loved and taken care of;
WORTHY of showing and expressing
my emotions and thoughts.

> I am worthy of
> being noticed.
> I am worthy of
> being imperfect.

I know that you cared so much about me.
It's because of you that I'm capable
of being in a place where
I NO LONGER need YOU.

Thank you...goodbye.

Poem 40: To My Son

I hope that one day
you don't hate me.
I hope that one day
you will see;

that I tried so hard
to do what was best for you,
and not what was
easiest for me.

I read ALL the books and
asked soo many questions!
What does the science say?
What is God's guidance?

I struggled to leave you crying…
I might've let TV become a habit.
I sang out my narrations daily.
Reading to you is Holy Ceremony.

> My promise to you:
> that my discomfort
> never outranks
> your best interest.

I can now see the struggles
of the generations preceding me,
but I don't feel their distance and
I don't understand their indifference.

How could any hand strike
that gorgeous gentle smile?
Tiredness could never justify
building in you any

—*rencor.*

I understand how anger in me
is a deep wound's response;
"Intergenerational Trauma,"
"Epigenetics," and so on…

but the pattern stops with me!
For you, I'll do whatever is best;
the chains will be Loosed,
I will be the last knot to unlace.

The threads will be well-kept.
You won't have to smile
if you don't feel like it.
I'll love you more than just

      —with my chest.

I'll keep reading the books,
and singing the songs,
and hoping you'll take longer naps,
when necessary, rock you in my lap.

——

I see for you a brighter future;
a stillness in your heart,
as one day you hold a little creature,
without having to set apart your heart.

I hope one day you still love me
and you see just how hard I tried,
to care more about your humanity,
than how loud you cried at night—

www.ingramcontent.com/pod-product-compliance
Lightning Source LLC
Chambersburg PA
CBHW071532120626
46550CB00006B/2419

* 9 7 8 1 9 6 6 6 5 5 5 0 3 *